Bible
Quiz Fun
For Everyone

by Shirley Beegle

STANDARD PUBLISHING
Cincinnati, Ohio

The puzzles in this book are based upon Scripture from the Holy
Bible, *New International Version*. Copyright © 1973, 1978, 1984
International Bible Society. Used by permission of Zondervan
Bible Publishers.

ISBN 0-87403-678-X

Table of Contents

Bible Occupations

Match the names with their occupations by writing the numbers in the appropriate spaces.

1. Aquila
   (Acts 18:2, 3)

2. David
   (1 Samuel 16:11, 13)

3. Deborah
   (Judges 4:4)

4. Cornelius
   (Acts 10:1)

5. Esther
   (Esther 2:17)

6. Caiphas
   (John 18:13)

7. Lydia
   (Acts 16:14)

8. Peter
   (Matthew 4:18)

9. Ruth
   (Ruth 2:2, 3)

10. Cain
    (Genesis 4:2)

11. Pilate
    (Matthew 27:11, 13)

12. Zacchaeus
    (Luke 19:2)

13. Paul
    (Acts 16:6)

14. Luke
    (Colossians 4:14)

15. Elijah
    (1 Kings 18:36)

_3_ prophetess

_5_ queen

_13_ missionary

_7_ seller of purple

_6_ high priest

_8_ fisherman

_11_ governor

_9_ gleaner

_14_ physician

_12_ tax collector

_1_ tentmaker

_2_ shepherd

_15_ prophet

_4_ centurion

_10_ farmer

Fathers and Sons

Match the fathers' names with their sons.

1. Adam
   (Genesis 4:1, 2)

2. Noah
   (Genesis 6:10)

3. Abraham
   (Genesis 16:15; 21:5)

4. Isaac
   (Genesis 25:24-26)

5. Jacob
   (Genesis 35:22b-26)

6. Nun
   (Joshua 1:1)

7. Amram
   (Numbers 26:59)

8. Boaz
   (Ruth 4:21)

9. Zebedee
   (Matthew 4:21)

10. Elkanah
    (1 Samuel 1:19, 20)

11. Jesse
    (1 Samuel 16:11-13)

12. Saul
    (1 Samuel 13:16)

13. David
    (2 Samuel 12:24)

14. Zechariah
    Luke 1:59, 60)

15. Kish
    (1 Samuel 9:1, 2)

_9_ James and John

_1_ Cain and Abel

_4_ Jacob and Esau

_2_ Ham, Shem, and Japheth

_8_ Obed

_7_ Moses and Aaron

_3_ Ishmael and Isaac

_14_ John the Baptist

_5_ Joseph and his 11 brothers

_12_ Jonathan

_15_ Saul

_13_ Solomon

_6_ Joshua

_10_ Samuel

_11_ David

Bible Authors

Match the clues with the authors' names.

1. He wrote most of the psalms.

2. He wrote five New Testament books.

3. He wrote 1 and 2 Peter.

4. He wrote 1 and 2 Timothy.

5. He wrote the book of James.

6. He wrote Ecclesiastes.

7. He wrote the first five Bible books.

8. He wrote most of the book of Proverbs.

9. He wrote Lamentations.

10. He wrote the book of Acts.

11. He wrote the first New Testament book.

12. He wrote the 65th book of the Bible.

13. He wrote most of the New Testament letters

14. He wrote the book of Revelation.

15. He wrote one of the Gospels, but he was not an apostle.

_3_ Peter

_6_ Solomon

_12_ Jude

_1_ David

_7_ Moses

_14_ John

_13_ Paul

_15_ Mark

_8_ Solomon

_9_ Jeremiah

_5_ James

_10_ Luke

_11_ Matthew

_4_ Paul

_2_ John

People and Animals

Match the people with animals associated with them.

1. David
    (1 Samuel 17:34)

2. Daniel
    (Daniel 6:16)

3. Rebekah
    (Genesis 24:15, 19)

4. Samson
    (Judges 15:4)

5. Elijah
    (1 Kings 17:6)

6. Jonah
    (Jonah 1:17)

7. Paul
    (Acts 28:3)

8. Balaam
    (Numbers 22:28)

9. Prodigal son
    (Luke 15:16)

10. Aaron
    (Exodus 32:4)

11. Abraham and Isaac
    (Genesis 22:13)

12. Noah
    (Genesis 8:8)

13. Jezebel
    (2 Kings 9:10)

14. Peter
    (Matthew 26:74, 75)

15. Pharaoh
    (Genesis 41:1-4)

4 foxes

6 large fish

9 swine

10 golden calf

11 ram

14 rooster

3 camels

5 ravens

13 dogs

12 dove

8 donkey

15 cows

2 lions

1 sheep

7 viper

Match Bible People and Bible Books

Match the people with the books that tell about them.

1. Samson   **4** 1 Samuel (9:1 ff.)

2. Esau and Jacob   **14** Esther (2:5–8:17)

3. Rahab   **9** Exodus (2:1 ff.)

4. King Saul   **1** Judges (13:2–16:31)

5. Boaz   **15** Philemon (10-19)

6. Shadrach, Meshach, Abednego   **7** Acts (6:5–7:60)

7. Stephen   **2** Genesis (25:24-26)

8. Queen of Sheba   **10** 2 Timothy (1:5)

9. Moses   **5** Ruth (2:1–4:13)

10. Eunice   **12** Luke (1:5-56)

11. Josiah   **6** Daniel (1:7)

12. Elizabeth   **3** Joshua (2:1-6)

13. Eliphaz, Bildad, Zophar   **8** 1 Kings (10:1-13)

14. Mordecai   **11** 2 Kings (22:1–23:30)

15. Onesimus   **13** Job (2:11-13)

Old or New Testament Stories

Circle the story in each group that does not take place in the Old Testament.

1. The story of the Wise-men, The fiery furnace, World destroyed by flood (Matthew 2:1-12).
2. Marching around Jericho, Ten lepers healed, The feast of Belshazzar (Luke 17:11-19).
3. The ax head that floated, Elijah fed by ravens, Dorcas raised from the dead (Acts 9:36-42).
4. Building of Solomon's temple, Betrayal for thirty pieces of silver, The valley of dry bones (Matthew 26:14-16).
5. Paul and Silas in jail, The story of baby Moses, Seven dips in the Jordan (Acts 16:16-39).
6. The Ten Commandments, The rich young ruler, The tower of Babel (Mark 10:17-22).
7. The burning bush, A dream about a ladder from earth to Heaven, The shipwreck of Paul (Acts 27:27-44).
8. Samson's haircut, The golden calf, The beginning of the church (Acts 2:37-47).
9. The coat of many colors, Stoning of Stephen, The witch of Endor (Acts 7:54-60).
10. Parable of the lost sheep, The contest on Mount Carmel, Crossing the Red Sea (Luke 15:3-7).
11. Famine in Egypt, The Sermon on the Mount, A dream about fourteen ears of corn (Matthew 5-7).
12. The baptism of Jesus, Slaying a giant, Selling a birthright (Matthew 3:13-17).
13. Feeding of the five thousand, The ten plagues, Woman turned into a pillar of salt (Matthew 14:15-21).
14. Locusts and wild honey, manna and quail, A preacher for Nineveh (Matthew 3:4).
15. Safe in a den of lions, Saul (Paul) blinded, birth of twins Esau and Jacob (Acts 9:1-9).

Who Doesn't Belong?

Cross out the names that do not belong.

1. Brothers: James and John, Philip and Bartholomew, Peter and Andrew.

2. Rulers: Herod, David, Bartimeus, Caesar Augustus.

3. Husband and wife: Zechariah and Elizabeth, Lazarus and Martha, Aquila and Priscilla.

4. Restored to life by Jesus: Lazarus, Jairus' daughter, Malchus.

5. Tax collectors: Thomas, Matthew, Zacchaeus.

6. Sisters: Mary and Martha, Elizabeth and Mary, Leah and Rachel.

7. Apostles who wrote Gospel books: Matthew, Mark, Luke, John.

8. Healed by Jesus: Bartimeus, ten lepers, Simeon.

9. Fathers of sons named James: Zebedee, Alpheus, Zechariah.

10. Fishermen: Thomas, Peter, James, Andrew.

11. Companions of Paul on his missionary journeys: John Mark, Barnabas, James, Luke.

12. Old Testament Kings: Solomon, Herod, Saul, Josiah.

13. Women in the book of Acts: Lydia, Dorcas, Mary Magdalene, Priscilla.

14. Books written by Paul: Romans, Jude, Galatians, Philemon.

15. Women in the book of Genesis: Eve, Sarah, Miriam, Rachel.

Old or New Testament People

*Write an **O** by the name if the person is in the Old Testament and an **N** by the name if the person is in the New Testament.*

——	1.	Elijah	——	31.	Thomas
——	2.	Zacchaeus	——	32.	Naaman
——	3.	Cornelius	——	33.	Rahab
——	4.	Jonathan	——	34.	Timothy
——	5.	Eve	——	35.	Jacob
——	6.	Paul	——	36.	Nicodemus
——	7.	Noah	——	37.	Pilate
——	8.	Ahab	——	38.	Sarah
——	9.	Rhoda	——	39.	Miriam
——	10.	Goliath	——	40.	Gideon
——	11.	Philip	——	41.	Abel
——	12.	Stephen	——	42.	Sapphira
——	13.	Jezebel	——	43.	Judas
——	14.	Ananias	——	44.	Naomi
——	15.	Moses	——	45.	Eunice
——	16.	Barnabas	——	46.	Barabbas
——	17.	Esau	——	47.	Rebekah
——	18.	Isaac	——	48.	Belshazzar
——	19.	Benjamin	——	49.	Herod
——	20.	Andrew	——	50.	Nathanael
——	21.	Mary	——	51.	Shadrach
——	22.	David	——	52.	Lazarus
——	23.	Dorcas	——	53.	Jesse
——	24.	Boaz	——	54.	Aaron
——	25.	Abraham	——	55.	Priscilla
——	26.	Elisha	——	56.	Onesimus
——	27.	Cain	——	57.	Methuselah
——	28.	Lydia	——	58.	Rachel
——	29.	Hannah	——	59.	Matthias
——	30.	Samson	——	60.	Deborah

Old Testament
Match the Numbers

Match the clues with the correct numbers.

1.	Days of Creation (Genesis 2:2)	2	11
2.	Joseph's brothers (Genesis 35:23-26)	4	8
3.	Days Joshua marched around Jericho (Joshua 6:3-5)	11	3
4.	People saved on ark (Genesis 7:13)	5	12
5.	Tribes of Israel (Genesis 49:28)	6	10
6.	Plagues (Exodus 7:14–11:10)	10	300
7.	Men cast into fiery furnace (Daniel 3:22, 23)	12	20
8.	Times Naaman dipped in Jordan River (1 Kings 5:13, 14)	13	969
9.	Days and nights Jonah was in the great fish (Jonah 1:17)	1	7
10.	Men in Gideon's army (Judges 7:7)	15	39
11.	Sons of Noah (Genesis 6:10)	7	3
12.	Pieces of silver received for Joseph (Genesis 37:28)	3	7
13.	Years Methuselah lived (Genesis 5:27)	14	40
14.	Days of rain when Noah was in the ark (Genesis 7:12)	9	3
15.	Books in the Old Testament	8	7

Old Testament Places

Match the clues with the Bible places.

1. Where God sent Jonah to preach (Jonah 3:2)
2. Country Joseph helped rule (Genesis 41:41)
3. Where Moses received the Ten Commandments (Exodus 19:20)
4. Adam and Eve's first home (Genesis 2:15)
5. David's hometown (1 Samuel 16:4, 13)
6. Ruth's homeland (Ruth 1:4)
7. Where Goliath was from (1 Samuel 17:4)
8. Where cedar trees for the temple came (1 Kings 5:6)
9. Where Jacob saw the vision of the ladder (Genesis 28:10-19)
10. Where Daniel was taken (Daniel 1:1, 6)
11. Where Abraham went to offer up Isaac (Genesis 22:2)
12. Where Noah's ark landed (Genesis 8:4)
13. Body of water through which Moses led the Israelites (Exodus 13:18)
14. Where Elijah had a contest with the prophets of Baal (1 Kings 18:19)
15. River where Naaman dipped to be healed of leprosy (2 Kings 5:10)

____ Bethlehem

____ Bethel

____ Mount Moriah

____ Nineveh

____ Moab

____ Lebanon

____ Egypt

____ Garden of Eden

____ Mount Sinai

____ Jordan

____ Mount Carmel

____ Gath

____ Babylon

____ Mount Ararat

____ Red Sea

Men in the Book of Genesis

Match the clues with the correct people.

1. He named the animals (2:19, 20).

2. God told him to build an ark (6:13, 14).

3. He was the first murderer (4:8).

4. He was put in charge of the whole land of Egypt (41:41).

5. He sold his birthright to his brother (25:29-33).

6. He was Joseph's youngest brother (35:18).

7. Joseph interpreted his dreams (41:25-32).

8. He was Rebekah's brother (24:29).

9. He bought Joseph from the Midianites, who had bought him from his brothers (37:28-36).

10. He was Abraham's nephew who journeyed to Canaan with Abraham and Sarah (12:4, 5).

11. He was the father of twelve sons (35:22).

12. He sent his chief servant back to his home country to find a wife for his son (24:1-4).

13. He was tricked into giving his blessing to Jacob instead of Esau (27:5-27).

14. He kept his brothers from killing their brother Joseph (37:21, 22).

15. He told the pharaoh that Joseph had interpreted his dream when he was in prison (41:9-13).

____ Isaac

____ Adam

____ Pharaoh

____ Noah

____ Benjamin

____ Cupbearer

____ Cain

____ Laban

____ Esau

____ Reuben

____ Abraham

____ Joseph

____ Potiphar

____ Jacob

____ Lot

Old Testament Who Said It?

Match the quotes with the people who said them.

1. "Let there be light" (Genesis 1:3).
2. "Am I my brother's keeper?" (Genesis 4:9).
3. "I know that my Redeemer lives" (Job 19:25).
4. "If I perish, I perish" (Esther 4:16).
5. "The Lord is my shepherd" (Psalm 23:1).
6. "Go, wash yourself seven times in the Jordan" (2 Kings 5:10).
7. "Speak, Lord, for your servant is listening" (1 Samuel 3:9).
8. "I have set my rainbow in the clouds" (Genesis 9:13).
9. "Who am I, that I should go to Pharaoh?" (Exodus 3:11).
10. "As for me and my household we will serve the Lord" (Joshua 24:15).
11. "So give your servant a discerning heart to govern your people" (1 Kings 3:9).
12. "The fire and wood are here, but where is the lamb for the burnt offering?" (Genesis 22:7).
13. "First sell me your birthright" (Genesis 25:31).
14. "You will not surely die" (Genesis 3:4).
15. "The Lord . . . will deliver me from the hand of this Philistine" (1 Samuel 17:37).

____ Jacob

____ David

____ Solomon

____ Job

____ Moses

____ Satan

____ Esther

____ God

____ Samuel

____ Isaac

____ David

____ Joshua

____ Elisha

____ Cain

____ God

Old Testament Relationships

Underline or circle the correct answers.

1. Adam and Eve were (husband and wife, father and daughter, son and mother) (Genesis 3:20).

2. Esau and Rebekah were (husband and wife, son and mother, brother and sister) (Genesis 25:25, 26).

3. Moses and Miriam were (father and daughter, brother and sister, son and mother) (Exodus 4:14; 15:20).

4. Solomon and Bathsheba were (son and mother, brother and sister, father and daughter) (2 Samuel 12:24).

5. Cain and Abel were (father and son, brothers, son and father) (Genesis 4:8).

6. Isaac and Sarah were (son and mother, father and daughter, brother and sister) (Genesis 21:3).

7. Abraham and Sarah were (son and mother, brother and sister, husband and wife) (Genesis 17:15).

8. Obed and Ruth were (brother and sister, husband and wife, son and mother) (Ruth 4:13, 21).

9. Saul and Jonathan were (brothers, son and father, father and son) (1 Samuel 14:42).

10. Joseph and Rachel were (brother and sister, son and mother, husband and wife) (Genesis 30:25).

11. Ham and Japheth were (father and son, brothers, son and father) (Genesis 6:10).

12. Ahab and Jezebel were (father and daughter, brother and sister, husband and wife) (1 Kings 21:4, 5).

13. Joseph and Benjamin were (brothers, son and father, father and son) (Genesis 35:24).

14. Moses and Zipporah were (son and mother, father and daughter, husband and wife) (Exodus 2:21).

15. Seth and Eve were (brother and sister, son and mother, father and daughter) (Genesis 4:25).

Match the Old Testament Verses

Match the two parts of these Bible verses.

1. "The earth is the Lord's, and everything in it, (Psalm 24:1)

2. "Remember your Creator in the days of your youth (Ecclesiastes 12:1)

3. "The heavens declare the glory of God; (Psalm 19:1)

4. "For to us a child is born, to us a son is given, (Isaiah 9:6)

5. "Your word is a lamp to my feet (Psalm 119:105)

6. "He was despised and rejected by men, (Isaiah 53:3)

7. "Trust in the Lord with all your heart, (Proverbs 3:5)

8. "I have hidden your word in my heart (Psalm 119:11)

9. "I know that my Redeemer lives, (Job 19:25)

10. "For the Lord is good and his love endures forever; (Psalm 100:5)

11. "But as for me and my house, (Joshua 24:15)

12. "Even though I walk through the valley of the shadow of death, (Psalm 23:4)

___ I will fear no evil."

___ we will serve the Lord."

___ that I might not sin against you."

___ before the days of trouble come."

___ and that in the end he will stand upon the earth."

___ and a light for my path."

___ the world, and all who live in it."

___ a man of sorrows, and familiar with suffering."

___ and the government will be on his shoulders."

___ his faithfulness continues through all generations."

___ the skies proclaim the work of his hands."

___ and lean not on your own understanding."

Old Testament Women

Match the clues with the women's names.

1.	Mother of Cain, Abel, and Seth (Genesis 4:1, 2, 25)	___ Sarah
2.	Mother of Isaac (Genesis 21:3)	___ Rebekah
3.	Mother of Jacob and Esau (Genesis 25:25, 26)	___ Jochebed
4.	Mother of Joseph (Genesis 35:24)	___ Bathsheba
5.	Queen of Xerxes (Ahasuerus) (Esther 2:16, 17)	___ Deborah
6.	Mother of Samuel (1 Samuel 1:20)	___ Eve
7.	Mother of Solomon (2 Samuel 12:24)	___ Miriam
8.	Sister of Moses (Numbers 26:59)	___ Dinah
9.	Mother-in-law of Ruth (Ruth 1:3, 4)	___ Hannah
10.	Sister-in-law of Orpah (Ruth 1:3, 4)	___ Rachel
11.	Mother of Moses (Numbers 26:59)	___ Ruth
12.	Wife of King Ahab (1 Kings 16:30, 31)	___ Naomi
13.	She had Samson's hair cut (Judges 16:18, 19)	___ Esther
14.	Daughter of Leah and Jacob (Genesis 30:20, 21)	___ Jezebel
15.	A prophetess and judge (Judges 4:4, 5)	___ Delilah

Old Testament Kings

Match the clues with the kings' names.

1. The father of King Saul
    (1 Samuel 9:1, 2)

2. David's father
    (1 Samuel 16:10-13)

3. Israel's first king
    (1 Samuel 10:21, 24)

4. The wisest king (1 Kings 4:29-34)

5. Played the harp for King Saul
    (1 Samuel 16:23)

6. Became king in Solomon's
    place (1 Kings 11:42, 43)

7. King of Babylon who saw
    a hand writing on the wall
    (Daniel 5:1, 5)

8. King of Israel who built a
    great temple to God
    (1 Kings 5:1-5)

9. Anointed Saul to be king
    (1 Samuel 10:1)

10. Dreams interpreted by Daniel
    (Daniel 2:27, 28)

11. King who stole a vineyard
    (1 Kings 21:16)

12. Father of Rehoboam
    (1 Kings 11:42, 43)

13. Became king when eight
    (2 Kings 22:1)

14. First ruler over ten tribes
    (1 Kings 11:31, 32)

15. Became king when seven
    (2 Kings 11:21)

____ Solomon

____ David

____ Belshazzar

____ Rehoboam

____ Jesse

____ Joash

____ Solomon

____ Nebuchadnezzar

____ Josiah

____ Kish

____ Solomon

____ Ahab

____ Jeroboam

____ Samuel

____ Saul

Old Testament Multiple Choice

Circle the correct answers to complete the sentences.

1. Shadrach, Meschach, and Abednego were friends of (David, Joseph, Daniel) (Daniel 1:6, 7).

2. Joseph helped rule the land of (Egypt, Judea, Galilee) (Genesis 41:41).

3. (Saul, Solomon, Ahab) was the first king of Israel (1 Samuel 11:15).

4. (Aaron, Joshua, Samuel) led the Israelites after Moses' death (Deuteronomy 34:9).

5. Ruth's mother-in-law was (Orpah, Hannah, Naomi) (Ruth 1:2-4).

6. (Jacob, Esau, Joseph) dreamed about a ladder that reached into Heaven (Genesis 28:10-12).

7. (Abraham's wife, Lot's wife, Jacob's wife) turned into a pillar of salt when she looked back at Sodom (Genesis 19:26).

8. (Aaron, Moses, Joshua) made a golden calf for the people to worship (Exodus 32:1-4).

9. When the Israelites were wandering in the wilderness God sent (biscuits and fish, manna and quail) for them to eat (Exodus 16:13, 31).

10. God appeared to Moses in a (burning bush, flower ing tree) (Exodus 3:2-6).

11. God sent down fire from Heaven to consume Elijah's sacrifice at the contest on (Mount Carmel, Mount Ararat, Mount Sinai) (1 Kings 18:19, 38).

12. God shut the lions' mouths when (David, Daniel, Isaiah) was put into their den (Daniel 6:21, 22).

13. God's people tried to build a tower to Heaven at (Bethel, Bethany, Babel) (Genesis 11:4-9).

14. His father gave (Joseph, Judah, Jacob) a coat of many colors (Genesis 37:3).

15. Baby Moses was found in the river by the (Pharaoh, Pharaoh's wife, Pharaoh's daughter) (Exodus 2:5, 6).

Which Are New Testament People?

Circle the names of the people that are in the New Testament.

1. Elijah, Zacchaeus, Cornelius, Jonathan.

2. Eve, Paul, Noah, Ahab.

3. Rhoda, Goliath, Philip, Stephen.

4. Jezebel, Ananias, Moses, Barnabas.

5. Esau, Isaac, Benjamin, Andrew.

6. Mary, David, Dorcas, Boaz.

7. Abraham, Elisha, Cain, Lydia.

8. Hannah, Samson, Thomas, Naaman.

9. Rahab, Timothy, Jacob, Nicodemus.

10. Pilate, Sarah, Miriam, Gideon.

11. Abel, Sapphira, Judas, Naomi.

12. Eunice, Barabbas, Rebekah, Belshazzar.

13. Herod, Nathanael, Shadrach, Lazarus.

14. Jesse, Aaron, Priscilla, Onesimus.

15. Methuselah, Rachel, Matthias, Deborah.

16. Apollos, Adam, Naboth, Samuel.

17. Lois, Aquila, Abel, Obed.

18. Solomon, Martha, John, Job.

19. Amram, Peter, Zebedee, Josiah.

20. Philemon, Daniel, Matthew, Mordecai.

Birth of Jesus Match-up

Match the clues in the first column with the answers in the second column.

1. He appeared to Mary
   (Luke 1:26, 27)   _____ Magi

2. Town where Jesus was born
   (Matthew 2:1)   _____ Joseph

3. Why Mary and Joseph went to
   Bethlehem (Luke 2:1-4)   _____ star

4. Where Wise-men were from
   (Matthew 2:1, 2)   _____ manger

5. King of Judea
   (Matthew 2:1)   _____ decree

6. There was no room there
   (Luke 2:7)   _____ shepherds

7. Another name for the Wise-men
   (Matthew 2:1)   _____ Nazareth

8. Jesus was laid in this
   (Luke 2:7)   _____ Mary

9. Mary's husband
   (Matthew 1:19)   _____ Gabriel

10. This led the Wise-men
    (Matthew 2:9)   _____ Savior

11. The first people to hear of Jesus'
    birth (Luke 2:8-12)   _____ inn

12. Mary and Joseph were from there
    (Luke 2:4, 5)   _____ east

13. What Caesar Augustus issued
    (Luke 2:1)   _____ census

14. A word describing Jesus
    (Luke 2:11)   _____ Bethlehem

15. Mother of Jesus
    (Matthew 1:18)   _____ Herod

New Testament Match the Numbers

Match the clues with the numbers.

1.	Thieves crucified with Jesus (Matthew 27:38)	____ 12
2.	Number of lost sheep (Luke 15:3)	____ 4
3.	Gifts from the Wise-men (Matthew 2:11)	____ 9
4.	Young women without extra oil for their lamps (Matthew 25:2, 3)	____ 1
5.	Jesus' apostles (Matthew 10:2)	____ 3
6.	Lepers who didn't thank Jesus (Luke 17:17)	____ 30
7.	Fishermen who became apostles (Matthew 4:18-22)	____ 40
8.	Jesus' age when He was baptized (Luke 3:23)	____ 27
9.	Pots of water Jesus changed to wine (John 2:6)	____ 3,000
10.	Days Jesus was in the wilderness during His temptation (Matthew 4:2)	____ 5
11.	People baptized on Day of Pentecost (Acts 2:41)	____ 5,000
12.	Times Jesus said we must forgive others (Matthew 18:22)	____ 2
13.	Men fed with five loaves and two fish (Matthew 14:21)	____ 77
14.	Times Peter denied Jesus (Luke 22:61)	____ 6
15.	Books in the New Testament	____ 3

Match the New Testament Verses

Match the two parts of these Bible verses.

1. "Come, follow me, and I will make you (Matthew 4:19)	____ that he gave his one and only Son."
2. "For God so loved the world (John 3:16)	____ as we also have forgiven our debtors."
3. "You are the Christ, (Matthew 16:16)	____ for they will see God."
4. "Forgive us our debts, (Matthew 6:12)	____ and on earth peace to men on whom his favor rests."
5. "Blessed are the pure in heart, (Matthew 5:8)	____ fishers of men."
6. "Do not judge, (Matthew 7:1)	____ the Son of the living God."
7. "Glory to God in the highest, (Luke 2:14)	____ on bread alone."
8. "It is written: Man does not live (Matthew 4:4)	____ or you too will be judged."
9. "But seek first his kingdom and his righteousness, (Matthew 6:33)	____ and preach the good news to all creation."
10. "Ask and it will be given to you; (Matthew 7:7)	____ No one comes to the Father except through me."
11. "Go into all the world, (Mark 16:15)	____ seek and you will find; knock and the door will be opened to you.
12. "I am the way and the truth and the life (John 14:6)	____ and all these things will be given to you as well."

New Testament Women

Match the clues with the women's names.

1. Sister of Mary and Lazarus
    (John 11:1, 2)   ____ Elizabeth

2. Mother of Jesus
    (Matthew 1:18)   ____ Lydia

3. Daughter of Lois
    (2 Timothy 1:5)   ____ Anna

4. Cousin of Mary
    (Luke 1:39, 40)   ____ Mary

5. Timothy's grandmother
    (2 Timothy 1:2, 5)   ____ Dorcas

6. Ananias' wife
    (Acts 5:1)   ____ Martha

7. Raised from dead by Peter
    (Acts 9:40, 41)   ____ Elizabeth

8. Seller of purple
    (Acts 16:14)   ____ Eunice

9. Prophetess at the temple
    (Luke 2:36)   ____ Lois

10. John the Baptist's mother
    (Luke 1:57, 60)   ____ Sapphira

11. Jesus raised her son from
    the dead (Luke 7:11-15)   ____ Priscilla

12. Wife of Felix
    (Acts 24:24)   ____ Widow of Nain

13. Aquila's wife
    (Acts 18:2)   ____ Mary

14. Servant girl
    (Acts 12:13)   ____ Drusilla

15. Mother of John Mark
    (Acts 12:12)   ____ Rhoda

Places in the Gospels

Match the clues with the Bible places.

1. Jesus' birthplace
   (Matthew 2:1)

2. Where Jesus grew up
   (Luke 2:51)

3. Where Jesus was baptized
   (Matthew 3:13)

4. Hometown of Mary and Martha
   (John 11:1)

5. Where temple was located
   (Luke 2:41, 46)

6. Country of woman at the well
   (John 4:5-7)

7. Place of Jesus' first miracle
   (John 2:11)

8. Where Zacchaeus lived
   (Luke 19:1, 2)

9. Another name for the Sea of Galilee
   (John 6:1)

10. On shore of Sea of Galilee
    (Matthew 4:13)

11. Peter, Andrew, and Philip's home-
    town (John 1:44)

12. Country King Herod ruled
    (Luke 2:1)

13. Where Jesus brought a widow's son
    back to life (Luke 7:11-15)

14. Where Jesus was crucified
    (Matthew 27:33)

___ Jordan River

___ Jericho

___ Bethlehem

___ Capernaum

___ Nain

___ Nazareth

___ Bethany

___ Bethsaida

___ Jerusalem

___ Judea

___ Golgotha

___ Tiberias

___ Samaria

___ Cana

Match Names for Jesus

Match the first and last parts of these names for Jesus.

1. Alpha
    (Revelation 1:8)

    ____ of Life

2. Beginning
    (Revelation 22:13)

    ____ and Last

3. Bread
    (John 6:35)

    ____ and Life

4. Bright and
    (Revelation 22:16)

    ____ and End

5. First
    (Revelation 1:17)

    ____ Shepherd

6. Good
    (John 10:11)

    ____ Morning Star

7. High
    (Hebrews 8:1)

    ____ and Omega

8. King
    (Revelation 17:14)

    ____ the World

9. Lamb of
    (John 1:36)

    ____ Priest

10. Light of
    (John 8:12)

    ____ of Peace

11. Lord of
    (Revelation 17:14)

    ____ God

12 Prince
    (Isaiah 9:6)

    ____ of Kings

13. Son
    (Matthew 14:33)

    ____ Lords

14. True
    (John 15:1)

    ____ of God

15. Way, Truth,
    (John 14:6)

    ____ Vine

Match Names of Jesus' Parables

Match the first and last parts of these names for some of Jesus' parables.

1.	Mustard (Matthew 13:31, 32)	____	Treasure
2.	Hidden (Matthew 13:44)	____	Servant
3.	Pearl of (Matthew 13:45, 46)	____	Sons
4.	Unmerciful (Matthew 18:23-25)	____	Virgins
5.	Two (Matthew 21:28-32)	____	Seed
6.	Wicked (Matthew 21:33-44)	____	Samaritan
7.	Ten (Matthew 25:1-3)	____	Great Price
8.	Good (Luke 10:25-37)	____	Fool
9.	Lost (Luke 15:4-7)	____	Tenants
10.	Rich (Luke 12:13-21)	____	Son
11.	Prodigal (Luke 15:11-32)	____	Sheep
12.	Great (Luke 14:16-24)	____	and Publican
13.	Pharisee (Luke 18:9-14)	____	Banquet
14.	Lost (Luke 15:8-10)	____	Manager
15.	Shrewd (Luke 16:1-13)	____	Coin

Life of Jesus Puzzle

Underline or circle the correct answers to complete the sentences.

1. Jesus was born in (Bethlehem, Jerusalem) (Matthew 2:1).

2. Jesus grew up in (Bethlehem, Nazareth) (Luke 2:51).

3. John baptized Jesus in the (Jordan River, Sea of Galilee) (Matthew 3:13).

4. Jesus was in the wilderness for (thirty days, forty days) during His temptation (Matthew 4:1, 2).

5. Jesus' first miracle was (changing water into wine, walking on the water) (John 2:1-11).

6. Jesus called (Matthew and John, James and John) to be disciples while they were mending their fishnets (Matthew 4:21).

7. The longest account of the Sermon on the Mount is in the book of (Matthew, Luke).

8. (Two, One) of the ten lepers Jesus healed returned to thank Him (Luke 17:15).

9. The people spread (garments and palm branches, flower blossoms) on the road when Jesus entered Jerusalem (Matthew 21:8).

10. The hometown of Jesus' friends, Mary, Martha, and Lazarus, was (Bethany, Bethphage) (John 11:1-3).

11. Jesus was crucified (beside one thief, between two thieves) (Matthew 27:38).

12. (Joseph of Arimathea, Nicodemus) buried Jesus' body in his tomb (Matthew 27:57-60).

13. (Mary the mother of Jesus, Mary Magdalene) was the first person to see Jesus after He arose from the dead (Mark 16:9).

14. Jesus ascended to Heaven (thirty days, forty days) after His resurrection (Acts 1:3).

15. (Andrew, Peter) tried to walk on the water to Jesus (Matthew 14:29, 30).

Jesus' Miracles

Match the clues with the correct answers.

1. What Jesus healed Bartimeus of (Mark 10:46)
2. Relative of a widow whom Jesus brought back to life (Luke 7:11-15)
3. An unusual place where Jesus told Peter to look for a coin (Matthew 17:27)
4. Jesus' first miracle (John 2:1-11)
5. Relative of Peter's whom Jesus healed (Matthew 8:14, 15)
6. Unusual way a sick man who was carried by four friends got into the house where Jesus was (Mark 2:3, 4)
7. Number of fish Jesus caused the apostles to catch after they fished all night and caught nothing (John 21:11)
8. Number of days Lazarus was dead before he was resurrected (John 11:39)
9. What Jesus said to the sea when he calmed it (Mark 4:39)
10. What Jesus did to a fig tree that had no fruit—only leaves (Matthew 21:19)
11. What Jesus told the blind man to do after He put clay on his eyes (John 9:7)
12. What the apostles said when they saw Jesus walking on the water to them (Matthew 14:26)
13. Number of loaves of bread Jesus used to feed the 5,000 (Matthew 14:19)
14. What Jesus told the ten lepers to do (Luke 17:14)
15. What happened to the swine into which Jesus cast devils (Matthew 8:32)

___ Four
___ Peace be still
___ A fish's mouth
___ Ran into the sea
___ Blindness
___ Mother-in-law
___ Changing water into wine
___ Five
___ Wash in the Pool of Siloam
___ Show themselves to priests
___ 153
___ Through the roof
___ Withered
___ Son
___ It is a ghost

Life of Christ Multiple Choice

Circle or underline the correct answers to complete the sentences.

1. Jesus went to (Jericho, Jerusalem, Bethlehem) when He was twelve years old (Luke 2:41-43).

2. Matthew was a (fisherman, carpenter, tax collector) when Jesus called him to follow Him (Matthew 9:9).

3. (Thomas, Philip, Thaddeus) said he wouldn't believe Jesus was alive until he touched the nail prints in His hands (John 20:24, 25).

4. Jesus fed 5,000 with (ten, five, seven) loaves and (one, two, three) fish (Matthew 14:16-21).

5. In the parable, the wise man built his house on (concrete, a cliff, rock) (Matthew 7:24).

6. Judas betrayed Jesus for (forty, thirty, twenty) pieces of silver (Matthew 26:14, 15).

7. After His resurrection, Jesus met two men on the road to (Emmaus, Jericho, Bethany) (Luke 24:13-32).

8. Jesus raised the daughter of (Cornelius, Jairus, Gamaliel) back to life (Mark 5:35-42).

9. Another name for Matthew was (Luke, Levi, Thomas) (Luke 5:27).

10. (Nathan, Nicodemus, Nathanael) came to see Jesus at night (John 3:1, 2).

11. Andrew brought his brother (James, Peter, John) to Jesus (John 1:40-42).

12. John the Baptist ate locusts and wild (strawberries, honey, cherries) (Matthew 3:4).

13. Jesus was born in the town of (Bethany, Bethel, Bethlehem) (Matthew 2:1).

14. John the Baptist baptized Jesus in the (Red Sea, Jordan River, Sea of Galilee) (Matthew 3:13).

15. (Matthew, Zacchaeus, Bartholomew) was not a tax collector.

Match Love Verses

Match the first and last parts of these Bible verses about love.

1. "Let us love one
    (1 John 4:7)

    ＿＿ is love."

2. "Love is
    (1 Corinthians 13:4)

    ＿＿ envy."

3. "God
    (1 John 4:16)

    ＿＿ His Son."

4. "Love . . . does not
    (1 Corinthians 13:4)

    ＿＿ love."

5. "Love is not easily
    (1 Corinthians 13:5)

    ＿＿ the world."

6. "God . . . loved us and sent
    (1 John 4:10)

    ＿＿ another."

7. "Love never
    (1 Corinthians 13:8)

    ＿＿ first loved us."

8. "Love your neighbor as
    (Matthew 19:19)

    ＿＿ enemies."

9. "We love because he
    (1 John 4:19)

    ＿＿ fails."

10. "The greatest of these
    (1 Corinthians 13:13)

    ＿＿ is love."

11. "God so loved the
    (John 3:16)

    ＿＿ angered."

12. "Love not
    (1 John 2:15)

    ＿＿ world."

13. "Fruit of the Spirit is
    (Galatians 5:22)

    ＿＿ yourself."

14. "If you love me,
    (John 14:15)

    ＿＿ patient."

15. "Love your
    (Matthew 5:44)

    ＿＿ you will obey
    what I command."

Jesus' Apostles

Match the clues with the apostles' names.

1. He was Peter's brother (John 1:40).   ____ Matthew

2. Another name for Matthew (Luke 5:27).   ____ Didymus

3. He betrayed Jesus (Matthew 26:47-49).   ____ James and John

4. He cut off Malchus' ear at the time of Jesus' arrest in the garden (John 18:10).   ____ Levi

5. Apostle with the longest name (Matthew 10:2-4).   ____ Andrew

6. They were called the sons of thunder (Mark 3:17).   ____ Zebedee

7. He tried to walk on the water to Jesus (Matthew 14:28-30).   ____ Judas

8. He had been a tax collector (Matthew 9:9).   ____ John

9. He denied knowing Jesus three times in one night (Matthew 26:69-75).   ____ Peter

10. He was the father of James and John (Matthew 4:21).   ____ Judas

11. Philip brought him to Jesus (John 1:45).   ____ Bartholomew

12. At His crucifixion, Jesus asked him to care for His mother (John 19:26, 27).   ____ Peter

13. Apostles Jesus took with Him into the garden to pray (Mark 14:33).   ____ Nathanael

14. He hanged himself (Matthew 27:5).   ____ Peter

15. Another name for Thomas (John 11:16).   ____ Peter, James, and John

Gospels Who Said It?

Match the statements with those who said them.

1. "Do this in remembrance of me" (Luke 22:19).

    ____ Prodigal son

2. "You are the Christ, the Son of the living God" (Matthew 16:16).

    ____ Leper

3. "I am innocent of this man's blood" (Matthew 27:24).

    ____ Satan

4. "Teacher, don't you care if we drown?" (Mark 4:38).

    ____ Zacchaeus

5. "If you are willing, you can make me clean" (Mark 1:40).

    ____ Pilate

6. "Repent, for the kingdom of heaven is near" (Matthew 3:2).

    ____ Nicodemus

7. "We know you are a teacher who has come from God" (John 3:2).

    ____ Angel

8. "Surely he was the Son of God!" (Matthew 27:54).

    ____ Judas

9. "Aren't you the Christ? Save yourself and us!" (Luke 23:39).

    ____ Centurion

10. "Where is the one who has been born king of the Jews?" (Matthew 2:2).

    ____ Peter

11. "Father, I have sinned against heaven and against you" (Luke 15:21).

    ____ Wise-men

12. "The one I kiss is the man" (Matthew 26:48).

    ____ Disciples

13. "Tell these stones to become bread" (Matthew 4:3).

    ____ Jesus

14. "He is not here; he has risen" (Matthew 28:6).

    ____ John the Baptist

15. "Look, Lord! Here and now I give half of my possessions to the poor" (Luke 19:8).

    ____ Thief on cross

New Testament Relationships

Circle or underline the correct answers to complete the sentences.

1. Zebedee and James were (brothers, father and son, son and father) (Matthew 4:21).

2. Timothy and Eunice were (son and mother, father and daughter, brother and sister) (2 Timothy 1:5).

3. Lazarus and Martha were (husband and wife, brother and sister, father and daughter) (John 11:1, 2).

4. Peter and Andrew were (brothers, father and son, son and father) (Matthew 4:18).

5. Aquila and Priscilla were (father and daughter, son and mother, husband and wife) (Acts 18:2).

6. Mary and Martha were (mother and daughter, sisters, daughter and mother) (John 11:1).

7. James and John were (father and son, son and father, brothers) (Matthew 4:21).

8. John Mark and Mary were (son and mother, father and daughter, brother and sister) (Acts 12:12).

9. Ananias and Sapphira were (father and daughter, brother and sister, husband and wife) (Acts 5:1).

10. Timothy and Lois were (grandson and grandmother, son and mother, father and daughter) (2 Timothy 1:5).

11. Zechariah and Elizabeth were (husband and wife, brother and sister, father and daughter) (Luke 1:5).

12. John the Baptist and Elizabeth were (father and daughter, son and mother, husband and wife) (Luke 1:57-60).

13. Joseph and Mary were (husband and wife, brother and sister, father and daughter) (Matthew 1:24).

14. Lazarus and Mary were (brother and sister, son and mother, father and daughter) (John 11:2).

15. John and Zebedee were (father and son, brothers, son and father) (Matthew 4:21).

Match the Animal, Vegetable, or Mineral

Match the clues with the correct answers.

1. Kind of food John the Baptist ate (Matthew 3:4)

2. Holy Spirit flew from Heaven as this after Jesus was baptized (Matthew 3:16)

3. Satan told Jesus to make them into bread (Matthew 4:3)

4. Soldiers put it on Jesus' head before He was crucified (Matthew 27:27, 29)

5. Kind of tree Zacchaeus climbed to see Jesus (Luke 19:4)

6. What John the Baptist's clothing was made of (Matthew 3:4)

7. What people spread on the ground as Jesus entered Jerusalem (Matthew 21:8)

8. What Jesus rode on during the triumphal entry (Matthew 21:7)

9. What the women took with them to Jesus' tomb (Luke 24:1)

10. What a woman had ten of and lost one (Luke 15:8)

11. A precious gift from the Wise-men to the baby Jesus (Matthew 2:11)

12. The kind of tree Jesus caused to wither (Mark 11:21)

13. In the parable of the sower, what represents the Word of God (Mark 4:14)

14. What Mary used to anoint Jesus' feet (John 12:3)

15. What Jesus used, besides five loaves of bread, to feed the 5,000 (John 6:9)

_____ Stones

_____ Gold

_____ Donkey – colt

_____ Camel's hair

_____ Garments and branches

_____ Oil

_____ Locusts and wild honey

_____ Sycamore

_____ Crown of thorns

_____ Seed

_____ Two fish

_____ Spices

_____ Dove

_____ Coins

_____ Fig

Who Spoke to Jesus?

Match the statements or questions with those who said them.

1. "Are you the king of the Jews?" (Matthew 27:11).
2. "I need to be baptized by you, and do you come to me?" (Matthew 3:14).
3. "You are the Christ, the Son of the living God" (Matthew 16:16).
4. "Look, Lord! Here and now I give half of my possessions to the poor" (Luke 19:8).
5. "If you are the Son of God, tell these stones to become bread" (Matthew 4:3).
6. "Here is a boy with five small barley loaves, and two small fish" (John 6:8, 9).
7. "Lord, if it's you, tell me to come to you on the water" (Matthew 14:28).
8. "Good Teacher, what must I do to inherit eternal life?" (Luke 18:18).
9. "Aren't you the Christ? Save yourself and us!" (Luke 23:39).
10. "Grant that one of these two sons of mine may sit at your right and the other at your left in your kingdom" (Matthew 20:21).
11. "My Lord and my God" (John 20:28).
12. "Surely not I, Rabbi?" (Matthew 26:25).
13. "Your father and I have been anxiously searching for you" (Luke 2:48).
14. "Master, Master, we're going to drown!" (Luke 8:24).
15. "Lord, don't you care that my sister has left me to do the work by myself? Tell her to help me!" (Luke 10:40).

—— Andrew
—— Pilate

—— Thief on cross
—— John the Baptist

—— Rich young ruler
—— Satan

—— Thomas
—— Peter
—— Zacchaeus
—— Peter
—— Mary
—— Disciples
—— Martha
—— Judas
—— Mother of James and John

To Whom Was Jesus Talking?

Match the statements or questions with those to whom Jesus said them.

1. _____ "This very night, before the rooster crows, you will disown me three times" (Matthew 26:34).
2. _____ "Let the little children come to me . . . for the kingdom of God belongs to such as these" (Luke 18:15, 16).
3. _____ "It is also written: Do not put the Lord your God to the test" (Matthew 4:5, 7).
4. _____ "Come, follow me, and I will make you fishers of men" (Matthew 4:19).
5. _____ "Your brother will rise again" (John 11:21, 23).
6. _____ "Unless a man is born again, he cannot see the kingdom of God" (John 3:1, 3).
7. _____ "Forgive them, for they do not know what they are doing" (Luke 23:34).
8. _____ "Come down immediately. I must stay at your house today" (Luke 19:5).
9. _____ "Put your finger here; see my hands. . . Stop doubting and believe" (John 20:27).
10. _____ "Are you betraying the Son of Man with a kiss?" (Luke 22:48).
11. _____ "Why were you searching for me? Didn't you know I had to be in my Father's house?" (Luke 2:49).
12. _____ "Were not all ten cleansed? Where are the other nine?" (Luke 17:17).
13. _____ "I tell you the truth, today you will be with me in paradise" (Luke 23:43).
14. _____ "Whoever drinks the water I give him will never thirst" (John 4:14).
15. _____ "Where shall we buy bread for these people to eat?" (John 6:5).

The apostles

Thomas

Judas

Nicodemus

Leper

Peter and Andrew

Thief on cross

Martha

Zacchaeus

Samaritan woman

Philip

Satan

Peter

God

Mary and Joseph

The Final Week

Match the clues with the correct people.

1. Peter cut his ear off (John 18:10)

2. The high priest who tried Jesus (John 18:24)

3. He was compelled to carry Jesus' cross (Luke 23:26)

4. He asked for Jesus' body so he could bury it in his own new tomb (Luke 23:50-53)

5. The first person to see Jesus after His resurrection (John 20:14-16)

6. Prisoner released when Jesus was crucified (Matthew 27:26)

7. Crucified on Jesus' right and left (Luke 23:32, 33)

8. Made a crown of thorns and put it on Jesus (Matthew 27:27-29)

9. Pronounced sentence for Jesus to be crucified (Matthew 27:24-26)

10. He said, "Surely this man was the Son of God" (Mark 15:39)

11. Told the women that Jesus had arisen (Matthew 28:5, 6)

12. Jesus sent them to find a donkey and her colt for His entry into Jerusalem (Matthew 21:1, 2)

13. Agreed to betray Jesus for thirty silver coins (Matthew 26:14-16)

14. He denied knowing Jesus three times in one evening (Matthew 26:69-75)

15. After Jesus' arrest, He was first brought to him (John 18:12, 13)

____ Angel

____ Barabbas

____ Joseph of Arimathea

____ Simon of Cyrene

____ Two thieves

____ Soldiers

____ Judas

____ Centurion

____ Mary Magdalene

____ Annas

____ Caiaphas

____ Peter

____ Malchus

____ Two disciples

____ Pilate

Book of Acts Multiple Choice

Circle or underline the correct answers to complete the sentences.

1. (Lydia, Dorcas, Priscilla) was a seller of purple (16:14).

2. Cornelius was a (general, guard, centurion) (10:1).

3. (Stephen, Peter, Philip) was the first Christian martyr (7:59, 60).

4. A man from (Ephesus, Europe, Macedonia) appeared to Paul in a vision (16:9).

5. (Stephen, Philip, Aquila) baptized a man from Ethiopia (8:27, 38).

6. (Silas, Luke, Timothy) was in the Philippian jail with Paul (16:22, 23).

7. Paul was shipwrecked on the island of (Patmos, Cyprus, Malta) (28:1).

8. Paul and Silas were freed from a prison in Philippi by (a fire, an earthquake, an angel) (16:26).

9. The church began on the Day of Pentecost in (Capernaum, Jerusalem, Nazareth) (2:5, 41).

10. When Paul was gathering wood on Malta a (dog, snake, fox) bit him but didn't hurt him (28:3).

11. (Rhoda, Mary, Dorcas) made clothes for widows and orphans (9:39).

12. Aquila and (Sapphira, Priscilla, Ruth) were tentmakers. (18:2, 3).

13. When Paul went to Rome, he lived in (a rented house, a tent, an inn) (28:30).

14. Peter was released from prison by (an angel, an earthquake, a tornado) (12:7-10).

15. (Luke, John, Barnabas) did not travel with Paul on a missionary journey.

Men in the Book of Acts

Match the clues with the men's names.

1. Priscilla's husband (18:2)

2. Escaped over the Damascus wall in a basket (9:24, 25)

3. Paul's companion on his first missionary journey (13:2, 3)

4. Healed a crippled man at temple gate Beautiful (3:6, 7)

5. First Christian martyr (7:54-60)

6. Saw a vision of a sheet with animals in it (10:9-12)

7. Cast a demon out of a girl in Philippi (16:16-18)

8. First Gentile who heard the gospel from Peter (10:24-48)

9. Imprisoned with Paul in Philippi (16:22, 23)

10. Paul restored him to life after he fell out of a window while Paul was preaching (20:9, 10)

11. Told Paul that he almost persuaded him to become a Christian (26:28)

12. King Herod had him killed with a sword (12:1, 2)

13. Young man who traveled with Paul on his second missionary journey (16:1-3)

14. Aquila and Priscilla "explained to him the way of God more adequately" (18:24-26)

15. Young man who started on the first missionary journey with Paul and Barnabas, but returned home (15:37)

____ Stephen

____ King Agrippa

____ Peter

____ Paul

____ Barnabas

____ Timothy

____ Peter

____ Paul

____ James

____ Silas

____ Cornelius

____ Eutychus

____ John Mark

____ Aquila

____ Apollos

Places in the Book of Acts

Match the clues with the Bible places.

1. Where Paul and his companions taught Lydia and her friends (16:12-15)

2. Where Paul lived with Aquila and Priscilla (18:1-3)

3. Paul's hometown (21:39)

4. Where Paul and Silas were in prison (16:12, 22, 23)

5. Where Paul saw an altar "To the Unknown God" (17:22, 23)

6. Where the church began (2:5, 41)

7. Where Paul had a vision and became blind (9:3-9)

8. Where Cornelius lived (10:1)

9. Town where Paul escaped over the wall in a basket (9:19, 25)

10. Where Dorcas was restored to life (9:36)

11. Where Paul was going when his ship was wrecked (23:11)

12. Where Demetrius, a silversmith, stirred up the craftsmen against Paul (19:17, 23-41)

13. Where the man whom Philip taught in a chariot was from (8:27)

14. Where Paul and Barnabas were called Mercury and Jupiter (14:8, 12)

15. City where Aquila and Priscilla taught Apollos (18:24-26)

____ Caesarea

____ Rome

____ Ephesus

____ Near Philippi

____ Ethiopia

____ Damascus

____ Corinth

____ Joppa

____ Tarsus

____ Jerusalem

____ Philippi

____ Lystra

____ Ephesus

____ Athens

____ Road to Damascus

Acts Who Said It?

Match the statements with those who said them.

1. "Do not hold this sin against them" (7:60). —— Philippian jailer

2. "I am now standing before Caesar's court where I ought to be tried" (25:10). —— Peter

3. "What must I do to be saved?" (16:30). —— Simon the Sorcerer

4. "Tabitha, get up" (9:40). ——

5. "Lord, I have heard many reports about this man and all the harm he has done to your saints in Jerusalem" (9:13). —— King Agrippa

6. "Repent and be baptized, every one of you in the name of Jesus Christ so that your sins may be forgiven" (2:38). —— Peter

7. "Do you understand what you are reading?" (8:30). —— Lydia

8. "Do you think that in such a short time you can persuade me to be a Christian?" (26:28). —— Peter and John

9. "If you consider me a believer in the Lord, come and stay at my house" (16:15). —— Ananias

10. "We cannot help speaking about what we have seen and heard" (4:20). —— Stephen

11. "Now we are all here in the presence of God to listen to everything the Lord has commanded you to tell us" (10:33). —— Paul

12. "Give me also this ability so that everyone on whom I lay my hands may receive the Holy Spirit" (8:19). —— Philip

—— Cornelius

Answers

Bible Occupations: 1-tentmaker. 2-shepherd. 3-prophetess. 4-centurion. 5-queen. 6-high priest. 7-seller of purple. 8-fisherman. 9-gleaner. 10-farmer. 11-governor. 12-tax collector. 13-missionary. 14-physician. 15-prophet.

Fathers and Sons: 1-Cain and Abel. 2-Ham, Shem, and Japheth. 3-Ishmael and Isaac. 4-Jacob and Esau. 5-Joseph and his 11 brothers. 6-Joshua. 7-Moses and Aaron. 8-Obed. 9-James and John. 10-Samuel. 11-David. 12-Jonathan. 13. Solomon. 14-John the Baptist. 15-Saul.

Bible Authors: 1-David. 2-John. 3-Peter. 4-Paul. 5-James. 6-Solomon. 7-Moses. 8-Solomon. 9-Jeremiah. 10-Luke. 11-Matthew. 12-Jude. 13-Paul. 14-John. 15-Mark.

People and Animals: 1-sheep. 2-lions. 3-camels. 4-foxes. 5-ravens. 6-large fish. 7-viper. 8-donkey. 9-swine. 10-golden calf. 11-ram. 12-dove. 13-dogs. 14-rooster. 15-cows.

Match Bible People and Bible Books: 1-Judges. 2-Genesis. 3-Joshua. 4-1 Samuel. 5-Ruth. 6-Daniel. 7-Acts. 8-1 Kings. 9-Exodus. 10-1 Timothy. 11-2 Kings. 12-Luke. 13-Job. 14-Esther. 15-Philemon.

Old or New Testament Stories: 1-The story of the Wise-men. 2-Ten lepers healed. 3-Dorcas raised from the dead. 4-Betrayal for thirty pieces of silver. 5-Paul and Silas in jail. 6-The rich young ruler. 7-The shipwreck of Paul. 8-The beginning of the church. 9-Stoning of Stephen. 10-Parable of the lost sheep. 11-The Sermon on the Mount. 12-The baptism of Jesus. 13-Feeding of the five thousand. 14-Locusts and wild honey. 15-Saul (Paul) blinded.

Who Doesn't Belong?: 1-Philip and Bartholomew. 2-Bartimeus. 3-Lazarus and Martha. 4-Malchus. 5-Thomas. 6-Elizabeth and Mary. 7-Mark, Luke. 8-Simeon. 9-Zechariah. 10-Thomas. 11-James. 12-Herod. 13-Mary Magdalene. 14-Jude. 15-Miriam.

Old or New Testament People: 1-O. 2-N. 3-N. 4-O. 5-O. 6-N. 7-O. 8-O. 9-N. 10-O. 11-N. 12-N. 13-O. 14-N. 15-O. 16-N. 17-O. 18-O. 19-O. 20-N. 21-N. 22-O. 23-N. 24-O. 25-O. 26-O. 27-O. 28-N. 29-O. 30-O. 31-N. 32-O. 33-O. 34-N. 35-O. 36-N. 37-N. 38-O. 39-O. 40-O. 41-O. 42-N. 43-N. 44-O. 45-N. 46-N. 47-O. 48-O. 49-N. 50-N. 51-O. 52-N. 53-O. 54-O. 55-N. 56-N. 57-O. 58-O. 59-N. 60-O.

Old Testament Match the Numbers: 1-7. 2-11. 3-7. 4-8. 5-12. 6-10. 7-3. 8-7. 9-3. 10-300. 11-3. 12-20. 13-969. 14-40. 15-39.

Old Testament Places: 1-Nineveh. 2-Egypt. 3-Mount Sinai. 4-Garden of Eden. 5-Bethlehem. 6-Moab. 7-Gath. 8-Lebanon. 9-Bethel. 10-Babylon. 11-Mount Moriah. 12-Mount Ararat. 13-Red Sea. 14-Mount Carmel. 15-Jordan.

Men in the Book of Genesis: 1-Adam. 2-Noah. 3-Cain. 4-Joseph. 5-Esau. 6-Benjamin. 7-Pharaoh. 8-Laban. 9-Potiphar. 10-Lot. 11-Jacob. 12-Abraham. 13-Isaac. 14-Reuben. 15-Cupbearer.

Old Testament Who Said It?: 1-God. 2-Cain. 3-Job. 4-Esther. 5-David. 6-Elisha. 7-Samuel. 8-God. 9-Moses. 10-Joshua. 11-Solomon. 12-Isaac. 13-Jacob. 14-Satan. 15-David.

Old Testament Relationships: 1-husband and wife. 2-son and mother. 3-brother and sister. 4-son and mother. 5-brothers. 6-son and mother. 7-husband and wife. 8-son and mother. 9-father and son. 10-son and mother. 11-brothers. 12-husband and wife. 13-brothers. 14-husband and wife. 15-son and mother.

Match the Old Testament Verses: 1-the world, and all who live in it." 2-before the days of trouble come." 3-the skies proclaim the work of his hands." 4-and the government will be on his shoulders." 5-and a light for my path." 6-a man of sorrows, and familiar with suffering." 7-and lean not on your own understanding." 8-that I might not sin against you." 9-and that in the end he will stand upon the earth." 10-his faithfulness continues through all generations." 11-we will serve the Lord." 12-I will fear no evil."

Old Testament Women: 1-Eve. 2-Sarah. 3-Rebekah. 4-Rachel. 5-Esther. 6-Hannah. 7-Bathsheba. 8-Miriam. 9-Naomi. 10-Ruth. 11-Jochebed. 12-Jezebel. 13-Delilah. 14-Dinah. 15-Deborah.

Old Testament Kings: 1-Kish. 2-Jesse. 3-Saul. 4-Solomon. 5-David. 6-Rehoboam. 7-Belshazzar. 8-Solomon. 9-Samuel. 10-Nebuchadnezzar. 11-Ahab. 12-Solomon. 13-Josiah. 14-Jeroboam. 15-Joash.

Old Testament Multiple Choice: 1-Daniel. 2-Egypt. 3-Saul. 4-Joshua. 5-Naomi. 6-Jacob. 7-Lot's wife. 8-Aaron. 9-manna and quail. 10-burning bush. 11-Mount Carmel. 12-Daniel. 13-Babel. 14-Joseph. 15-Pharaoh's daughter.

Which Are New Testament People?: 1-Zacchaeus, Cornelius. 2-Paul. 3-Rhoda, Philip, Stephen. 4-Ananias, Barnabas. 5-Andrew. 6-Mary, Dorcas. 7-Lydia. 8-Thomas. 9-Timothy, Nicodemus. 10-Pilate. 11-Sapphira, Judas. 12-Eunice, Barabbas. 13-Herod, Nathanael, Lazarus. 14-Priscilla, Onesimus. 15-Matthias. 16-Apollos. 17-Lois, Aquila. 18-Martha, John. 19-Peter, Zebedee. 20-Philemon, Matthew.

Birth of Jesus Match-up: 1-Gabriel. 2-Bethlehem. 3-census. 4-east. 5-Herod. 6-inn. 7-Magi. 8-manger. 9-Joseph. 10-star. 11-shepherds. 12-Nazareth. 13-decree. 14-Savior. 15-Mary.

New Testament Match the Numbers: 1-2. 2-1. 3-3. 4-5. 5-12. 6-9. 7-4. 8-30. 9-6. 10-40. 11-3,000. 12-77. 13-5,000. 14-3. 15-27.

Match the New Testament Verses: 1-fishers of men." 2-that he gave his one and only Son." 3-the Son of the living God." 4-as we also have forgiven our debtors." 5-for they will see God." 6-or you too will be judged." 7-and on earth peace to men on whom his favor rests." 8-on bread alone." 9-and all these things will be given to you as well." 10-

seek and you will find; knock and the door will be opened to you." 11-and preach the good news to all creation." 12-No one comes to the Father except through me."

New Testament Women: 1-Martha. 2-Mary. 3-Eunice. 4-Elizabeth. 5-Lois. 6-Sapphira. 7-Dorcas. 8-Lydia. 9-Anna. 10-Elizabeth. 11-Widow of Nain. 12-Drusilla. 13-Priscilla. 14-Rhoda. 15-Mary.

Places in the Gospels: 1-Bethlehem. 2-Nazareth. 3-Jordan River. 4-Bethany. 5-Jerusalem. 6-Samaria. 7-Cana. 8-Jericho. 9-Tiberias. 10-Bethsaida. 11-Capernaum. 12-Judea. 13-Nain. 14-Golgotha.

Match Names for Jesus: 1-and Omega. 2-and End. 3-of Life. 4-Morning Star. 5-and Last. 6-Shepherd. 7-Priest. 8-of Kings. 9-God. 10-the World. 11-Lords. 12-of Peace. 13-of God. 14-Vine. 15-and Life.

Match Names of Jesus' Parables: 1-Seed. 2-Treasure. 3-Great Price. 4-Servant. 5-Sons. 6-Husbandman. 7-Virgins. 8-Samaritan. 9-Sheep. 10-Fool. 11-Son. 12-Supper. 13-and Publican. 14-Coin. 15-Steward.

Life of Jesus Puzzle: 1-Bethlehem. 2-Nazareth. 3-Jordan River. 4-forty. 5-changing water into wine. 6-James and John. 7-Matthew. 8-One. 9-garments and palm branches. 10-Bethany. 11-between two thieves. 12-Joseph of Arimathea. 13-Mary Magdalene. 14-forty days. 15-Peter.

Jesus' Miracles: 1-Blindness. 2-Son. 3-A fish's mouth. 4-Changing water into wine. 5-Mother-in-law. 6-Through the roof. 7-153. 8-Four. 9-Peace be still. 10-Withered. 11-Wash in the pool of Siloam. 12-It is a spirit. 13-Five. 14-Show themselves to priests. 15-Ran into the sea.

Life of Christ Multiple Choice: 1-Jerusalem. 2-tax collector. 3-Thomas. 4-five, two. 5-rock. 6-thirty. 7-Emmaus. 8-Jairus. 9-Levi. 10-Nicodemus. 11-Peter. 12-honey. 13-Bethlehem. 14-Jordan River. 15-Bartholomew.

Match Love Verses: 1-another." 2-patient." 3-is love." 4-envy." 5-angered." 6-His Son." 7-fails." 8-yourself." 9-first loved us." 10-is love." 11-world." 12-the world." 13-love." 14-you will obey what I command." 15-enemies."

Jesus' Apostles: 1-Andrew. 2-Levi. 3-Judas. 4-Peter. 5-Bartholomew. 6-James and John. 7-Peter. 8-Matthew. 9-Peter. 10-Zebedee. 11-Nathanael. 12-John. 13-Peter, James, and John. 14-Judas. 15-Didymus.

Gospels Who Said It?: 1-Jesus. 2-Peter. 3-Pilate. 4-disciples. 5-Leper. 6-John the Baptist. 7-Nicodemus. 8-Centurion. 9-Thief on cross. 10-Wise-men. 11-Prodigal son. 12-Judas. 13-Satan. 14-Angel. 15-Zacchaeus.

New Testament Relationships: 1-father and son. 2-son and mother. 3-brother and sister. 4-brothers. 5-husband and wife. 6-sisters. 7-brothers. 8-son and mother. 9-husband and wife. 10-grandson and grandmother. 11-husband and wife. 12-son and mother. 13-husband and wife. 14-brother and sister. 15-son and father.

Match the Animal, Vegetable, or Mineral: 1-Locusts and wild honey. 2-Dove. 3-Stones. 4-Crown of thorns. 5-Sycamore. 6-Camel's hair. 7-Garments and branches. 8-Donkey — colt. 9-Spices. 10-Coins. 11-Gold. 12-Fig. 13-Seed. 14-Oil. 15-Two fish.

Who Spoke to Jesus?: 1-Pilate. 2-John the Baptist. 3-Peter. 4-Zacchaeus. 5-Satan. 6-Andrew. 7-Peter. 8-Rich young ruler. 9-Thief on cross. 10-Mother of James and John. 11-Thomas. 12-Judas. 13-Mary. 14-Disciples. 15-Martha.

To Whom Was Jesus Talking?: 1-Peter. 2-The apostles. 3-Satan. 4-Peter and Andrew. 5-Martha. 6-Nicodemus. 7-God. 8-Zacchaeus. 9-Thomas. 10-Judas. 11-Mary and Joseph. 12-Leper. 13-Thief on cross. 14-Samaritan woman. 15-Philip.

The Final Week: 1-Malchus. 2-Caiaphas. 3-Simon of Cyrene. 4-Joseph of Arimathea. 5-Mary Magdalene. 6-Barabbas. 7-Two thieves. 8-Soldiers 9-Pilate. 10-Centurion. 11-Angel. 12-Two disciples. 13-Judas. 14-Peter 15-Annas.

Book of Acts Multiple Choice: 1-Lydia. 2-centurion. 3-Stephen. 4-Macedonia. 5-Philip. 6-Silas. 7-Malta. 8-an earthquake. 9-Jerusalem. 10-snake. 11-Dorcas. 12-Priscilla. 13-a rentedhouse. 14-an angel. 15-John.

Men in the Book of Acts: 1-Aquila. 2-Paul. 3-Barnabas. 4-Peter. 5-Stephen. 6-Peter. 7-Paul. 8-Cornelius. 9-Silas. 10-Eutychus. 11-King Agrippa. 12-James. 13-Timothy. 14-Apollos. 15-John Mark.

Places in the Book of Acts: 1-Near Philippi. 2-Corinth. 3-Tarsus. 4-Philippi 5-Athens. 6-Jerusalem. 7-Road to Damascus. 8-Caesarea. 9-Damascus. 10-Joppa. 11-Rome. 12-Ephesus. 13-Ethiopia. 14-Lystra. 15-Ephesus.

Acts Who Said It?: 1-Stephen. 2-Paul. 3-Philippian jailer. 4-Peter. 5-Ananias. 6-Peter. 7-Philip. 8-King Agrippa. 9-Lydia. 10-Peter and John. 11-Cornelius. 12-Simon the Sorcerer.